THE ART OF
COMMUNICATION

How to Inspire and Motivate Success Through Better Communication

---

Peter Oliver

THE ART OF COMMUNICATION

Copyright © 2018 by Concise Reads™

All rights reserved. No part of this publication may be reproduced in any form or by any means without the prior written permission of the publisher or author.

DISCLAIMER: The author's books are only meant to provide the reader with the basic knowledge of a certain topic, without any warranties regarding whether the reader will, or will not, be able to incorporate and apply all the information provided. Although the author and publisher have made every effort to ensure that the information in this book was correct at press time, the author and publisher do not assume and hereby disclaim any liability to any party for any loss, damage, or disruption caused by errors or omissions, whether such errors or omissions result from negligence, accident, or any other cause.

TABLE OF CONTENTS

1. INTRODUCTION
2. STRUCTURING THE CONTENT
3. STRUCTURING THE DELIVERY
4. KNOW YOUR AUDIENCE
5. BE INSPIRING
6. BE ENGAGING
7. BONUS: HOW PEOPLE CONNECT
8. BONUS: THE TED SECRET FORMULA FOR PUBLIC SPEAKING

INTRODUCTION

"To effectively communicate, we must realize that we are all different in the way we perceive the world and use this understanding as a guide to our communication with others" -- Tony Robbins

Tony Robbins, famous author and life coach, makes the point that communicating has to take into account the audience. This seems simple enough, but take a minute and think about how often you considered the other person or people whom you are addressing.

The truth is we try but we don't really try. We communicate in a way that we think is obvious and straightforward for us.

The majority of disagreements are because of bad communication---Yes, bad communication! When someone is perceived boring, condescending, insulting, charismatic, charming, or even insightful it is because of the what and how they communicate. If the meaning of your message depends on how the audience perceives it, then I don't know about you but I agree with Tony Robbins--you must internalize this understanding and let it guide your communication.

Ok, so you'll take into account other people's perception. You'll walk a mile in their shoes and all that and for what? Well, for the love and admiration of the people of course. Imagine how many great adjectives can be said about you? Wouldn't it be grand? I suppose it would be grand if your job in life was to be loved and your success and daily income depended on you being loved. However, to make **powerful communication** more applicable to the everyday peter or joe, we need to deconstruct this just one more step.

If your purpose in life is to be liked and loved by the people, then you are using communication as a tool to **motivate action**. Communication has also been said to be an effective tool to raise awareness through information--which ideally should result in some form action.

Good. So communication is a tool used for the purposes of **motivating action**. Done. But how is one motivated to act? Well you need to **understand** the content, and then you need to be **inspired** to act. That's it.. In this concise read, you'll learn how to be a powerful communicator like Steve Jobs when he convinced the world to pay as much as they did for a phone in 2007.

Homework: Find that video online and watch as he take something that at the time was completely foreign-- given we never used our index finger to swipe anything except pick our nose back then--and turns it into an easily understandable, convincingly revolutionary, and ironically a crucial identity differentiator between the iphone users and the non-adopters. Ofcourse, keep in mind that you will be watching the video with the lens of someone more than a decade in the future, so expect to be slightly biased, but still enjoy the art in his **content** and **delivery** and how that **inspired** you to **act** (buy). We'll next talk about content and delivery.

If you couldn't find the video, here is a youtube link < https://youtu.be/MnrJzXM7a6o>. Listen to how he describes the iPhone as "an ipod, a phone, and an internet communicator".

STRUCTURING THE CONTENT

You may have heard helpful comments about how long or how short your communication is whether prior to a company presentation, or before sending that company-wide email. Length is important but not as important as you think.

You must think of your content as a menu item at a successful fast food joint. The customer always wants to know what is popular or what are the top 3 items. Then, they want to know where to go to find more information. This additional information could be a list of alternative items like 'vegan' or 'gluten free' just below the more popular greasy items OR it could be a nice footnote that says 'Ask for the special of the day'. This is what the fast food aficionado wants and you must oblige!

To structure the content in a way that is most useful to the listener, we need to adopt what's known as the **pyramid principle**. It is also known as the **iceberg principle**. Think of the shape of a pyramid and break it into three layers. Imagine that your conclusion is the smallest stone all the way at the top and that conclusion is supported by stones underneath it in two layers.

The <u>first layer</u> underneath is the direct evidence that ultimately proves the conclusion. The <u>second layer</u> is the evidence that supports the assumptions. Of course it can be as many layers as you want but the point is that it is layered--that is to say that if someone wants to understand a layer, you offer the evidence in the layer below (the direct evidence) and <u>you don't overshare</u>

additional information that will only confuse the message if the message is intended to motivate action. For simplicity just remember **three layers** as they are known in the industry:

1. Conclusion OR key argument OR governing thought
2. Direct evidence OR supporting key statements
3. Supporting evidence OR Facts OR assumptions

Always remember the goal of communication- -to motivate action.

Your intention to motivate action requires you to start with your conclusion and then build supporting arguments or show compelling evidence. That's why it is called the pyramid principle.

Barbara Minto, a Harvard MBA, developed the pyramid principle and offers an in depth book (for about $135) and an online course to help solidify this technique. The pyramid principle is a top-down approach in contrast to scientific literature that starts with an introduction, then the methods, then the results, and finally the conclusion. Consequently, many people who use the pyramid principle think that it is a new concept.

It's not.

You see, people in general only absorb information if they are seeking it out. If they are the ones asking 'why?' then they are more likely to pay attention. And people always ask 'why?'. Simon Sinek, author of *Start With Why* stresses that successful companies or successful ideas have discovered their why, and employees who work in those companies or people who buy their product resonate with that *why*. His focus is more on motivating the action of buying a product or idea but what I'd like you to understand is that he is also stressing that how the message is communicated is important.

The link to his TED talk is as follows < https://www.ted.com/talks/simon_sinek_how_great_leaders_inspire_action>. If the link is broken, simply google it.

If everyone cares about the *why*, then let's use scientists as example. These are folks who are used to reading communication in the form of introduction, methods, results, and conclusion. If scientists were truly presented with the introduction first, they would seldom read past it. This was discovered a long time ago and that is why every scientific article must have an abstract. Granted the abstract has the same order of information but it gets to the conclusion faster (literally in less than a minute) and the scientist is left wondering 'why?'. If the conclusion caught their interest, then they would proceed to read the entire article to answer their question.

Similarly, the purpose of starting with the conclusion is to cause your audience to ask 'why?'

As soon they do, then you have their attention and you have them engaged.

Side story: There was once a very tall, very handsome, and extremely charismatic CEO. Everyone loved listening to him speak. He was motivational, inspirational, and enigmatic when it came to giving speeches. The problem he later found out was that each audience member had a different version of the conclusion he intended to make. He couldn't control the content of the message because he was leading with emotional intelligence (EQ), which is important but only equally important to content. My team worked with the CEO to focus on the structure of his content, providing the conclusion first, the evidence second, and the assumptions or supporting material last. A second attempt and a second round of speeches later, the audience all took away the same clear and concise message.

Practice applying the pyramid principle in every form of communication. This isn't a $135 book, but you really only need the affordable version to get started. Remember to practice this in your email content as well.

Avoid the extremes of putting all your facts and key statements in a long email as well as treating email like it was an instant message with a one line response.

Other principles are:
- Don't be mysterious in the subject line. Instead of 'follow up' say 'follow up notes from meeting x this afternoon'
- Write your <u>governing thought</u> in the first few lines, keep pleasantries to a minimum

- Write a few <u>key statements</u>, no more than three to support your governing thought
- Structure the key statements or facts in bullet points so 'visually' it appears as the foundation or supporting evidence of the argument in the first sentence
- Leave room to connect offline (i.e. Happy to discuss on the phone)
- Keep the whole email to one screen size (i.e. don't make your reader scroll, that's the first trigger for disengagement).
- Never participate in an email chain of more than 4 emails. After that, pick up the phone or if you're in a less formal organization, join slack or another medium for instant or real-time communication.

STRUCTURING THE DELIVERY

> "Persuasion is achieved by the speaker's personal character when the speech is so spoken as to make us think him credible. We believe good men more fully and more readily than others: this is true generally whatever the question is, and absolutely true where exact certainty is impossible and opinions are divided."
>
> -- Aristotle

In design theory, designers typically map out a user journey with sticky notes on the wall. They use this method to help them with <u>story lining</u> or building the narrative.

They then start deciding how this ordered information will be shown to the user. Will it be a pop-up? Or a side alert? They put their vision on a wireframe or sketch it out. This view of how it looks like is called the storyboard.

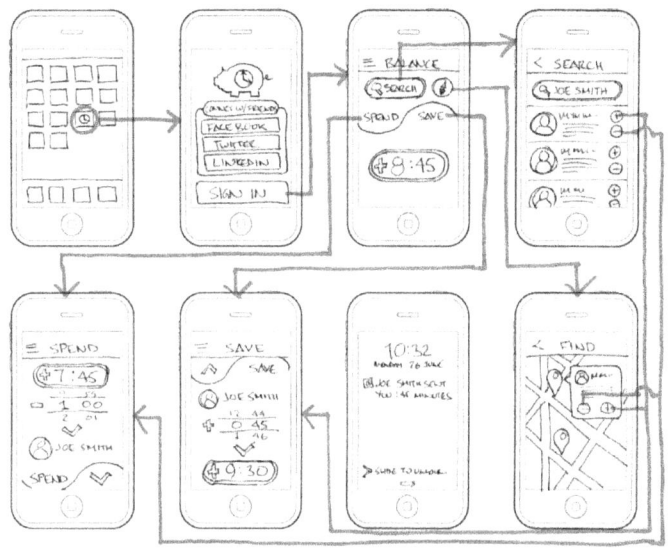

Finally, the designer then decides on the design elements like color, shape of the buttons, fonts, etc. This is known as the assets used.

In learning to structure the delivery of effective communication, we borrow from designers these three elements:

1. Storyline
2. Storyboard
3. Assets

Let's go through a simple example. You want to pitch your startup or company project proposal. You have your pyramid all ready to go with the governing thought, the key statements that support the governing thought, and the facts that support the key statements. Great! Presenting a pyramid is boring. So you think to yourself, how can I deliver my content in a way that will inspire your boss or investors to take action? First you decide on your storyline. You think that providing context in the form of a problem statement will grab their attention. Then you would offer the solution which is your governing thought, followed by your supporting key statements, and then end with a compelling one liner conclusion that de-risks the situation. Your storyline might look something like this:

1. Problem: People love listening to music but they don't want to pay for it.
2. Solution: Startup Streamify will offer free streaming music paid for by advertisements.
3. Supporting arguments: users have become accustomed to online advertisements on blogs, websites, and even within their apps.
4. Supporting argument 2: The number of pirated music has skyrocketed in the last 3 years and shows no signs of slowing down.
5. Supporting argument 3: The quality of pirated music is so poor that given the opportunity to stream high quality

    music, millions of users who pirate
    music will now enjoy it for free
6. Conclusion: Not only do we offer
    music lovers something they want for
    free, but we get paid seamlessly and the
    major music labels save millions in lost
    revenue by opting in to discounted
    revenue from streaming.

This is a fictional case, and typically an actual investor pitch will use the competitive landscape, financials, etc as supporting arguments for why their solution will be a success and possibly 'disruptive'. I remember an advertisement of an old woman falling down the stairs and trying to reach for the phone but oh no it's too far away--but wait now with the sensor 3000 wristband she can call for help with the press of a button. I'm sure the product has saved many lives, but the point I'm illustrating is that startup pitches and marketing pitches practice the method of **storylining** and so should you when you want to communicate effectively.

So now you have your storyline for your brand new startup, Streamify. Next, you need to decide on the **storyboard**. The purpose of the storyboard is to visualize how you will present your content for maximum effect. By visualizing the end product, you inherently end up deciding what to emphasize and what to deprioritize. In the case we've been using above, we've decided to use a powerpoint presentation as our channel or medium to present our content. We then might decide to create a page with giant numbers in red to emphasize the millions lost due to pirated music for supporting argument 2. For our conclusion we might draw out the different stakeholders in a pie-chart and show that the pirated music has now been redistributed to us and the music labels in exchange for a much lower royalty fees for streaming content. A win-win situation that is clearly visualized.

Powerpoints are just one channel. If you have one solution that solves a diverse group of problems, then a series of images can be presented in sequence or put up along the conference room. Each image is a problem that can be solved with your solution. Think of an art gallery showcasing one artist's work. Each painting is a piece of the story, and art lovers walk around until they find the piece of art that resonates with them. This is what's known as a <u>gallery walk</u> in the business world. Now you have an engaged audience member who wants to find out what the solution is that can solve this one problem they care about. In addition to gallery walks, consider video presentations, or bringing in actual people who've used your product, or a live demonstration--which is by the way what Steve Jobs did when he pitched his company's new 'iphone' to Vodaphone.

There isn't much to say on assets except that the what we described above like charts and visuals are assets and that there are some additional helpful things you can do improve the delivery of your message such as building a one page executive summary that outlines your story and printing it out in crisp contrasting font or sending it ahead of the presentation to prime the audience members on the order of your story.

One pet peeve of mine that I want to share with all---never use bright light colors on white pages, and make sure your power point only uses sans serif font that is at least 14px.

KNOW YOUR AUDIENCE

"To effectively communicate, we must realize that we are all different in the way we perceive the world and use this understanding as a guide to our communication with others" -- Tony Robbins

We see the previous Tony Robbins quote again on purpose. Understanding who your audience is factors into structuring the **content** and **delivery** of your message. Would you present your scientific research the same way to a group of scientists as you would to a third grade class? This is rhetorical, but it's ok if you answered it. Marketers know that segmenting and targeting is playbook advertising 101. They know their message cannot appeal to everyone so they have to tailor it to a specific target audience. Our unlucky presidents unfortunately can't do the same even though they try by choosing venues that are highly targeted like a steel factory or a university because their message can be tailored better. Still, when they give national speeches you can figuratively hear half the nation moaning or groaning regardless of who the president is. Still, speech writers are clever and help tailor the message so it tries to appeal to the majority.

You really have to factor your audience into structuring the content and delivery of your message. I'm repeating myself to emphasize how important this is.

The easiest way to know your audience is to spend 5 minutes on a piece of paper and write down who the **stakeholders** are, or in other words who your audience is. If it's a small group then list individually, and if it's a large group then organize by some common theme like the sales department and marketing department will be in the audience and they are two separate stakeholders. Next, write down the **current mindset** of the stakeholder as it is related to your message. Two things are important when writing out their current mindset:

1. What are their values or beliefs, and
2. How much do they understand or know regarding your message.

Next write down what **change in mindset** you hope to achieve. Be realistic here. You are not going to convince meat lovers to become vegan, at least not after the first presentation.

Understanding your audience and describing their current and post presentation mindset goal will help you tailor your **storylining** and **storyboard** so that it is an effective presentation.

A great example is when President Kennedy was trying to sell his vision of 'a man on the moon'. He tailored his speech to Rice University, repeating multiple times the pronoun 'you' when he stated that students are needed to make this vision a reality--to literally put a man on the moon. His speech motivated a whole generation of Houston graduating students to apply to NASA. In fact, his tailored speeches promoting his vision were so motivational that during a visit to the NASA space center in 1962, he saw a janitor carrying a broom and wondered what he was doing at NASA to which the janitor replied "I'm helping put a man on the moon."

BE INSPIRING

Word choice and choice of visual plays a very important role. In fact, the diligence of practicing a speech over and over isn't meant to internalize the content but rather to internalize the meaning of the content. The more you practice, the more you will find that you develop natural pauses during your speech because of the profound meaning of your choice of words. It is therefore easily concluded that great speakers are the ones who can connect with their audience's emotions using the same content as mediocre speakers who just read the text on their powerpoint page.

To be inspiring you need to believe in your message and explain with passion, enthusiasm, and conviction. It is easy for me to tell you that you should stress buzzwords, pause after a thought provoking statement, or to infuse your message with a personal story. It is harder to sound convincing if you don't <u>internalize</u> the meaning of your message.

So the first step is to practice conveying the message with the <u>same emotion</u> that you had when you first structured the content.

The second step is to add rhetorical techniques such as repeating key words or statements, using powerful visuals to elicit emotion and engage your audience, and using analogies that the audience can relate to.

Martin Luthor King Jr's 1963 speech on capitol hill was full of imagery, repetition, pauses, and the use of the personal pronoun. Read the full speech in the government archives or listen to it online. Here is a quote from that speech:

"I have a dream that my four little children will one day live in a nation where they will not be judged by the color of their skin but by the content of their character. I have a dream ... "

Rhetoric is not as most of us believe to mean political rhetoric infused with hot air. Rhetoric is simply one part of three that constitute the art of discourse. In ancient Greece, children were taught the three components of discourse which are grammar, logic, and rhetoric and which were part of the traditional classical education. Rhetoric or the output combined with powerful logic (in our case with the pyramid principle) inspired people into action. Rhetoric without content is what we're used to watching on late night news channels.

Rhetoric is a very powerful tool and one that takes a lot of practice to fine tune. Obama's signature hand gesture and long pauses are his form of rhetoric and it's proven effective. It made him sound very presidential and he intended it that way through late nights of exhaustive speech practice. No one is born with Rhetoric. A human raised by wolves acts like a wolf. A man or woman immersed in watching and delivering speeches soon becomes well versed in the techniques of rhetoric.

BE ENGAGING

There are many studies out there that show the majority of people believe an effective communicator is one who has presence. If you pick up a men's or women's magazine, you'll see the same message stated differently in that people are initially attracted to how you look (which includes your presence) rather than what comes out of your mouth.

Presence it turns out also plays a role in building trust with the audience and giving the audience the confidence to take action. Presence is how you stand up straight, the choice of clothes, how you project your voice, whether you make eye contact, among other behavioral and non-verbal communication.

Presence is your style of communication.

Presence is simply stated the ability to be completely comfortable and relaxed without any nervous jitters. Feeling completely at ease takes practice.

A simple life hack is to expand your body by using the superman or wonder woman power pose for 2 minutes with your arms out, your chest out, and your back straight. 2 minutes of pretending to be bigger than you are changes your body chemistry enough to convince you that you are taller, stronger, bolder, and braver than you were just a few minutes ago.

The tonality of your voice is important and also signals whether you are comfortable and aligned with the meaning of your message and the emotional state of your audience. NEVER use disclaimers, caveats, or qualifiers.

NEVER. It completely destroys the intended effect of presence. I've seen this happen in both the oral and written form too many times by junior associates who hope to someday become leaders, but their caveats and qualifiers lose the trust of the senior leadership especially if used frequently.

A simple life hack here is to project your voice and then bring it down to a much lower volume and slower pace. Do that for 2 minutes and you will find that during speech time there is much less resistance to modulating your voice. You'll notice some speakers have an almost muffled quiet monotone voice during a presentation. Those are the folks who rarely speak outside of having to give these business presentations. 2 minutes of practice and your body has been recently reminded that it can modulate the voice even in stressful environments.

Your non-verbal communication is important.

We've learned a great deal on non-verbal communication in the 'Art of Negotiation' Concise Reads. An important additional point here is that your non-verbal behavior is in reaction to your audience's emotional state. This requires some EQ on your part in understanding if the audience is engaged, confused, bored, angry and at which parts of your speech these emotional states exist. If they are engaged, you should straighten your back and raise your hands in emphasis. If they are confused, you should try to make eye contact with as many members as possible while also over emphasizing your expressions.

Reread this section and write down a few takeaways to practice every day.

BONUS: HOW PEOPLE CONNECT

There's no secret sauce. I'm just reminding you what you already know but forget that human connections are a two way street. You need to practice the same positive behaviors you expect from others. These behaviors are most commonly found during communication, that I thought they would be helpful to include here.

Six of the most common ways to form a connection with someone are as follows:

1. **Research their background:** often times a conversation can feel like an interview when we know nothing about a person. If there is an opportunity to learn something about your audience

beforehand then use their background to guide their conversation. People always enjoy it when someone has a genuine interest in them

2. **Mimic their behavior:** mimicking is the utmost form of flattery. If someone uses a colloquial word to describe something, go ahead and use the same word. If they are sitting, go ahead and sit and do the same if they are standing. Mimicking allows your audience to feel comfortable.

3. **Be an engaged listener:** we oftentimes hear what someone is saying and then jump to the next topic. That is disrespectful. <u>Listen</u>, <u>absorb</u>, <u>synthesize</u>, and then respond to what you heard. Active listening (and

reacting to what you heard) keeps the audience engaged.

4. **Pause at the right moments**: often times someone tells us something controversial or profound and we find ourselves reacting right away. Wait. Pause. Show your audience that you are synthesizing. Use affirmative words like "that makes sense" or "Interesting, I haven't thought of that before". Also pause when you rattle off long speeches. Pause and ask "what do you think?" or "Have you had a similar experience?".

5. **Be genuinely interested:** if you convince yourself to be genuinely interested, and you convince yourself that everyone has an interesting story to tell, then you will find that the conversation will flow very easily

because your curiosity will cause you to find out more.

6. **Don't match stories:** When one person tells a story that the other has also experienced, they blurt out what their experience has been and it becomes a battle of who has the best stories. Both parties leave thinking to themselves "geez, the ego on that person". In other words, don't talk about yourself without being prompted or asked to. If the other person is interested they will ask, and if you simply can't resist the urge just say "I've had something similar happen to me" then PAUSE and see if they want to hear more. They may not be interested in your particular storyline. That's ok. Move on to another topic if they're not interested to continue the

dialogue on the topic you're interested in.

7. **Be kind:** This is a golden rule. People are all suffering and talk to enough people and you'll hear their suffering comes out in their stories or their commentary. People who are not greeted with kindness, feel uncomfortable quickly and fall silent at the very moment when a supportive "Oh that must have been hard" is all it would have taken to relieve the suffering. Remember, acknowledging one's suffering rather than silently ignoring it is what forms a real connection. The 'if you have nothing good to say don't say anything at all' is not helpful, because at the same time 'silence speaks a thousand words'.

BONUS: THE TED SECRET FORMULA FOR PUBLIC SPEAKING

Available at < https://youtu.be/-FOCpMAww28 >. If the link is broken, just google it.

TED curator Chris Anderson shares this secret.

1. The premise is that there is a collective consciousness that understands ideas when presented in a construct of building blocks.

2. The single purpose of a TED speaker is to share an idea in a construct that allows the conscious mind to relate it to its world view and ultimately absorb it.

3. Focus on one major idea and deconstruct it into all its attributes and building blocks. This includes using visual or emotional examples to put the idea into context.

4. Stir your audience's curiosity. Humans by nature crave balance. When you present a disconnect between their world view and your idea, they will naturally want to solve that disconnect and are thus primed to participate in active listening.

5. Build your idea using concepts your audience already understand. Use assumptions that your audience understand to build your argument. Use metaphors. Lead them to that Aha moment one building block at a time.

6. Make your idea worth sharing. This is a consequence of understanding your stakeholders and the relevance of your idea. This is effectively knowing the 'why?'.

Good luck, and pick up your next copy of Concise Reads to acquire new lessons and skills in business.

--The End--

www.ingramcontent.com/pod-product-compliance
Lightning Source LLC
Chambersburg PA
CBHW050246230526
45470CB00005B/2131